Audition & Book It!

Audition & Book It!

HELEN MCCREADY, C.S.A.

Copyright © 2011 by Helen McCready

Hollywood Entertainment Publishing
Burbank, CA 91505

ISBN: 978-0-578-07517-4

Printed in the United States of America

Contents

For my three beautiful children
Wes, Helen, & Bobby
who are my greatest accomplishments

About the Author

HELEN McCready, C.S.A., a Canadian citizen, began working as an actor in 1985 in Vancouver, British Columbia. She started out as an extra on the hit TV show "21 Jump Street" as well as assisted in extra casting at the Denise Love Talent Agency. She moved to Arizona in 1994 where she continued her career working as a casting director assistant.

In 1999, Helen launched Helen Wheels Productions, LLC in Arizona. Since then, her company has successfully been expanding into other states and Canada.

Now residing in North Hollywood, California, Helen's success as a casting director has continued with projects such as Director Sam Mendes's "Away We Go" and did some of the additional casting in Nancy Meyer's - Meryl Streep's and Alec Balwdwin's 2010 "It's Complicated".

In 2010 Helen McCready has been head casting director for a number of films including the soon to be hit "Zombie drugs" and "Suspicion" a Thriller/Drama. As well as working on big budget and independent films, Helen has seen the potential of new talent that comes through in exciting productions for the internet known as a "web series". She is currently casting two SAG "web series" one extremely popular and disturbingly interesting, "The Resolve", and a brand new project, "Writers Block".

Upcoming 2011, Helen will take charge of many projects, such as "Unrest", a Horror movie, and "Margarine Wars", both with massive potential and are already attracting "A-lister" movie stars. Eight other feature films are scheduled to be cast in 2011 not including other feature films that Helen is "in talks with".

Helen McCready is also Vice President of casting for two other independent production companies.

In light of being an accomplished C.S.A Casting Director, Helen has also explored the world of writing and completing projects where she has been credited as writer and producer.

Recently, Helen completed a screenplay for a film entitled, "Racetrack" that is currently in pre-production stage. "Racetrack" is loosely based on the real life events of her father. Helen will be an executive producer, writer, and casting director for this feature film.

Helen has ventured into the world of reality TV and is producing an original concept in a pilot show called "Callback". "Callback" is a reality television comedy show filming actors competing for a supporting role in a feature film. Episodes will involve various challenges and scenarios that professional actors are confronted with every day.

Unafraid of change or challenges, Helen has embraced the social networking sites with open arms such as Facebook, Twitter, Linked-In, Meet-Up, Yelp, IndieGoGo, to name a few. With email and the social media, it makes the whole casting process much quicker, simpler, and a fantastic new way to reach out to the talent. It's brilliant!" as stated by Helen McCready in a recent television interview.

For current information please go to her websites at:
www.HelenMcCready.com
www.helenwheels.net
www.AuditionAndBookIt.com

CHAPTER ONE

The Five Elements
of a Winning Audition

O **NE** thing I find as a casting director is that the toughest thing I see talent do when they come into the audition room is struggle to keeping their dialogue "real". I see it over and over again and the solution is simple. You can do this by using your energy. Talent must keep their energy up and keep the audition piece they are doing "real" but cannot confuse the two.

Energy is NOT over-acting! When you over-act, or push the dialogue, you push us away from believing your character. You didn't keep it "real". When I see actors do an audition that lacks energy, I am ready to see the next actor waiting to audition; it's that simple. Energy is the emotional connection an actor brings to his or her character.

So, how do you have great energy and keep the audition piece real or believable? By using the five elements I have come up with for this book and in my teachings.

I love actors! They are an amazing breed of talent that

wants to come in and just give us their all. Sometimes, by giving us your all, it looks like you are pushing your acting or which is what is referred to as "overacting". Talk as you would talk in everyday conversation. Your energy is so important. You have to forget about the words on the script and bring your energy and emotional choice to the page. Actors will see the words on the page and think, "Oh I have to punch that word -- that really is an important word!" When that choice is made, the scene does not come out right because the actor is forcing a choice, not trusting their emotional choice to carry them through. Think of the famous line Jack Nicholson does in "A Few Good Men" when he yells, "You can't handle the truth!". I would guarantee he was not thinking about punching the word 'handle' or 'truth'…it just came out through his emotional choice.

The words really do not matter – it's what you do with them that count. The work has already been done for you by the writer. It is your job to bring those scripted words to life so that your audience (producer, director, casting director or whoever might be in the room) believes you are that character.

When you get your sides, you have 5 things to decide: Who you are, where you are, what the conflict of the scene is, what is your relationship with the other characters in the scene, and what is your emotion choice or choices.

1. Who am I?
    It is vital that you know exactly who you are in the

scene. Sometimes, it is not very specific when you are given the sides for your audition. Use what you know about the character! You will have received a breakdown of who you are but there is going to be so much more in the dialogue. Read and re-read the sides. Ask yourself questions. Where am I from? What is my background? Am I aggressive or passive? (Passive is usually not a strong choice; passive choices can come across as low energy), who am I in this scene? The more questions you ask of yourself, the more you can connect to the character.

2. Where am I?

   You MUST know where you are in the scene! If the sides do not tell you, make it up. You have to be grounded and know exactly where you are to create a believable character. It will also help you to take yourself out of the audition room and put yourself in a place that only your character can relate to. Again, ask questions. Where am I? Why am I here? How did I get here? Do I like being here? Am I in a hurry to leave or do I want to stay? Connect your character to a location and be as specific as possible. The more specific you are, the more believable you will be in your scene.

3. What is the relationship?

   Most sides that you will get will have another

character in the scene. You will either be told the relationship with this character or you will need to figure it out from the sides you have been given. Is the relationship father/daughter? Mother/son? Husband/wife? Girlfriends? Boyfriends? Co-workers? Your boss? Again, be specific. Our emotional thoughts change depending on the relationship with another person. I definitely feel differently towards my girlfriend than I do my sister or my producer. Each relationship will strike up a different emotion. This is critical if you want us to believe in you and your audition.

4. What is the emotion of the character?

    This is the paramount of the five elements. The emotional choices you make will carry the whole scene. Think of it as a thought process. Every time you think of any thought it creates an emotional reaction. Think of a newborn baby. What emotion does that bring? Think of that terrible day, September 11, 2001. What emotion does that bring? Think about winning the lottery. What emotion does that bring? Are you getting my point? If you think the thought behind the dialog, the emotion will come right to you.

    Now, the thought that you have may not be what the dialog is in the scene. For example, let's say your character doesn't like the other character in the scene and your line is: "Gee, looks like we will be working together for awhile." What is your character really thinking? Probably something like, "I can't stand you and I hope you get fired". Think about both those lines. You can see where the emotional choice can be quite different depending on your thought behind the dialogue, which will make what you really need to say in the script a stronger emotional choice that fits the scene. So while you are saying the line, "Gee, looks like we will be working together for awhile" but you're thought is, "I can't stand you and I hope you get fired", the emotion behind the thought will be anger (possibly...you have many choices but we'll keep it simple for now), therefore, you will know to deliver the line angry and to feel the emotion of anger. Then you go to the next line and go through the same process. Trust this system and you will give us a great emotional audition! You have to have a strong emotional commitment or we won't believe you. No scene can survive if the emotional intensity and energy lays flat and dormant. Don't just say the lines; know why you are saying them and how they make your character feel so you can project during your audition.

5. What is the conflict?
   Every scene has conflict, otherwise we would get bored watching the movie or television show.

What is at stake for your character? If you cannot find it, you will absolutely bore us. You must find the substance in the scene. The best way to do this is decide what or where was your character prior to this scene? Where does your character plan on going when the scene is over? Why are you here now? Be specific and then trust your instincts! Try to look for where the scene is changing. If it is a good script, something is moving the scene forward and you need to find it. Once you figure it out, you will find the conflict in the scene. That being said, you will have times where you will think, "I absolutely cannot find the conflict in this scene!" Why? Because sometimes the intensity of the scene is making the character change, not the conflict. This happens very often in dramas and love stories. Not every scene is an argument, however, every scene will have its level of intensity and you can use this in place of conflict. You will absolutely find one or the other and when you do, you will be able to build your character, emotional choices, level of your emotional choices, and your energy around it.

Don't drop your energy on any line. You have got to be sure and give 100% of every word you speak or it will show that you either don't know what you are doing or cannot bring the right energy to the scene. Do every line with confidence. Confidence sells! And when you are in the audition room, you are your only sales person, so sell yourself to us with your confidence and skills. Whatever choice you make, commit to it.

If you make the right choices, using the 5 elements it will always work. You just have to trust the system. It's all about the energy and keeping it real. More scripts get re-written on set or during production because when the actor brings their gift into the scenes it can change everything. Directors want the actor to bring life to the character. That is your job as an actor!

Don't rush the scene. Actors tend to talk too fast, maybe because of nerves, but whatever the reason, slow down and study the pace of the scene. The moments in between the lines can be the best moments of the whole scene. Don't ever feel pressured to rush. Remember the old rule, "Silence is golden" – acting is probably the number one place for this rule. The acting you do when you are not speaking is just as important as when you are speaking. Use those moments to draw us into you.

CHAPTER TWO

Your Headshot and Resume Are Your Marketing Tool

WIKIPEDIA defines a **headshot** as: "A headshot is a photographic technique where the focus of the photograph is a person's face." It does not say hands, arms, body shot, hats, dangling earrings, props...you get the idea. We want to see your face!

1. Why is my headshot important?

   The first thing a casting director always asks for, before seeing any talent, is the headshot and resume. Why? Because it all starts with the look. The "look" can be anything from a young Redford type to a 90 year old, overweight grandma and everything in between, but the selection starts with seeing if you look like the character breakdown. This is your most value piece of marketing material you will invest in for your career.

   First impressions are everything in this town and it

starts with your headshot! I'm sure you have heard this a thousand times yet time and time again, I see headshots from talent that either do not come close to looking like themselves or they choose to let a "friend" take their photo to save on money and, guess what, you get what you pay for! I cannot stress enough how important it is to have a professional photographer take your headshot. This does not mean it will cost you thousands of dollars and if that is what a photographer is charging, then run! Your headshots should only cost you $200-$400 for two different looks; your commercial shot and theatrical shot.

Actors will take their headshots, staple it to their resumes for auditions, casting calls, etc. It is imperative that your headshot looks like you and it lets us see who you are – we should get a very good feel as to what your personality is like and see individuality. And remember it is called a "head"shot…we want to see your head! Do not send in your comp cards, if you have modeled, or full body shots; we need to see you. Some actors will shoot a ¾ shot, which is okay but not for the first impression. Show us your face! And in this day of digital age, we are looking at thumbnail pictures first, so if you use a ¾ shot your face is going to be extremely small and you could very easily be overlooked. We need to see your eyes. It's your eyes that are going to sell us, not your body! Your eyes must convey to us that you have a good grasp of yourself and who you are: confident, positive, distinctive. Make sure to keep your hands out of the shot. Again, we want to see your face and especially your eyes, not how nice your fingernails are groomed.

2. Why are character shots important?

   Character shots are headshots of you portraying other roles/characters you feel you can portray. Below is a talent with different character shots, along with his commercial and theatrical shot. Each one tells me exactly who he is and how his look speaks clearly where I could cast him. (Left to Right: TOP: Theatrical, teenage bully, nerd, BOTTOM: commercial/fun, sweet teenager, ¾ Theatrical).

   These shots let me know exactly what I am getting and who is going to walk through my audition room door.

   If you don't know your character type, start watching television shows or movies and see where you might see yourself. Ask yourself, "Could I do that role?" If the answer is yes (and be honest with yourself) you will start to find out who you are as an actor. It's also important to know your age range. For instance, the headshot of the actor below would not submit for anything over 20 years of age or younger than 16 years, so his age range is 16-20 years. Most age ranges are within 4 to 5 years. Rarely, if ever, does an actor have a ten year age range, so again, be honest with yourself when looking in the mirror to figure it out. When in doubt, ask your agent or another industry professional.

3. What should I wear?

   Wear something you love to be seen in. You should bring several shirts or tops to your photo shoot that make you feel confident and whatever else would describe your character as shown in the headshots above. Make sure that whatever you bring is either nicely pressed or dry cleaned because every little crease will show up in your headshot. Do not bring loud prints or crazy, bright colors. You do not want your clothes distracting so that our eyes go to your shirt before we see your face. Solid colors are always the optimum choice. Choose colors that look good on you. Black and white is always good to bring for at least one option. Ladies, do not wear big dangly or large earrings. They become as distracting as big bold prints. Not wearing any jewelry at all is the best option.

4. How do I take a good headshot?
   This is easy…have fun and bring on a good attitude! Do not think about the end result or that you are even having your photograph taken. Look at the lens as if it is your best friend; try NOT to see it as a camera. Relax. Enjoy the moment. Try to be as natural as you can. This should be effortless. If you need to, have a friend take a ton of digital photos of you JUST for practice, so you can focus on looking into the lens and have focus on having fun with it. If you are uptight or nervous, it will show in your headshot and I've seen plenty of those over the years and those actors are not getting

called in and probably do not even understand why.

Be sure to get a good night's sleep so you can wake up feeling happy and ready to have an exciting day getting your headshots done! After all, this is what is going to get your foot in the door to book a job! Just as discussed in the previous chapter, about your energy in the audition room, you have to have that same type of energy for your photo shoot. And no fresh haircuts, please! If you need a haircut prior to your shoot, book it a week before. You do not have a natural look with a fresh haircut; it actually becomes distracting in your photo.

5. What do I do with my headshot once I have it?
    The first thing you should do is see if anything needs to be touched up and that does not mean wrinkles, freckles, birthmarks, moles etc. If these are part of your look then be proud of them! I've had actors submit headshots when the breakdown called for someone in their twenties and a forty year old walks in the room. Two problems with this: (1) they have wasted both our time because they obviously will NOT get the job and (2) they are missing out on the opportunities that are out there for forty year olds because their headshot looks like they are twenty. You MUST look like YOU in the headshot. Whatever your headshot represents had better walk in the audition room. It

is okay to touch up possible make-up smudges, a hair that is streaming across your face or awkwardly in the photo, etc. - anything that does not take away from who you really are.

The next step is to get an agent, which is not an easy task, but not impossible. Make sure your headshot is in an email format/size and start sending it out with your resume. Attach them both and have a cover letter to use for the email. At some point, someone will want you to come in and audition, so be ready with a monologue (we will cover that in an upcoming chapter). Also, submit yourself for everything you can. Search online and find the projects to submit yourself for – I will talk about the different online services and social media in a later chapter.

Once you have an agent they will submit your headshots to the network and studio projects that you are unable to find in any breakdown service, but do not stop submitting for yourself! Your agent gets 10% of your paycheck which means you still need to do 90% of the work.

The most important thing to remember in this chapter is that everything is going to start with your headshot. That is your calling card to get through a casting director's door and into the audition room.

What is the proper format for my resume?

On the next page is a template for you to use when setting up your resume. This is industry standard.

What is worth mentioning here is the *billing on a resume. Most actors tend to put the name of the character instead of their billing for their work in film and television. We are not interested in the character – we want to know how another project cast you; it is extremely attention-grabbing to us!

If you are not sure, it is as follows:

> *Billing is the role type, not the character's name.*

FILM BILLINGS: Lead, supporting, day player, featured (NO EXTRA WORK, PLEASE!)

TELEVISION BILLINGS: Series regular, recurring, guest star, co-star, featured (NO EXTRA WORK, PLEASE!)

YOUR NAME HERE

WWW.YOURWEBSITEHERE.COM

UNION AFFILIATIONS HERE

Agency or logo	Voice Mail or Cell__
Contact: 555-555-5555	Email Address Here
Hair: Brown	Height: 0'0"
Eyes: Brown	Weight: 000 lbs

FILM

Project Title	Billing	Prod Co./Director
Project Title	Billing	Prod Co./Director
Project Title	Billing	Prod Co./Director

TELEVISION

Project Title	Billing	Prod Co./Network
Project Title	Billing	Prod Co./Network
Project Title	Billing	Prod Co./Network

THEATRE

Project Title	Character	Theatre Name
Project Title	Character	Theatre Name
Project Title	Character	Theatre Name

COMMERCIALS

List Available Upon Request

TRAINING

School Name	Class/Workshop	Instructor Name
School Name	Class/Workshop	Instructor Name
School Name	Class/Workshop	Instructor Name

SPECIAL SKILLS

Accents and/or Dialects: Spanish (native), German
Accent, Dancing: Ballet, Jazz, Swing, Tango,
Ballroom, Tap, Fold, Square, Special Talents: Juggling,
Impressions, Stand-up Comedy, Public Speaking,
Singing, Musical Instruments: Piano, Sports: Golf,
Horseback Riding, Fencing

CHAPTER THREE

The Audition Room – Part One – First Impressions

IT might help if you first know the responsibilities of a casting director.

A casting director is a middle-man (or more likely a middle-woman) who finds the actors needed to fill roles in movies, television shows, theatrical productions, commercials or even music videos.

The studio, producers, director and writers are on one side, and the actors and talent agents on the other -- with the casting director in the middle. "Middle-woman" applies because casting directors represent one of the few entertainment occupations that's dominated by women, not men [source: Chinoy and Jenkins].

A casting director's responsibilities extend beyond contacting actors or agents and holding auditions. Casting directors assemble casts that may include hundreds of actors, negotiate deals with the actors' agents and manage the contracts once the actors have signed.

Casting directors become involved in pre-production.

The casting director may be employed by the studio, work for a casting company or, an independent casting director, such as myself.

The casting director:

- Meets with the producers, the director and possibly the writer to understand the project.
- Meets with the production accountant for information about the casting budget, the money that'll be used to pay the actors.
- Reads the script and make notes about all the speaking parts.
- Creates a list of possible actors, in preferred order, for the most important parts first.
- Contacts the actors or their agents to determine their availability provides the list to the producers and director to make their decision. *List actors (the stars) may not be asked to audition.*
- Prepares lists of actors and production schedule for supporting and more minor actors.
- Makes appointments for auditions or readings with the available actors.
- Provides information about available parts to talent agencies and lists opportunities with Breakdown Services, a company that maintains a daily list of acting opportunities.
- Conducts auditions.
- Makes recommendations, based on auditions, for

each speaking part *The director and producers make the final selections.*

- Negotiates contracts with the actors' agents, keeping an eye on the casting budget.
- Issues casting calls for minor acting parts and conducts those auditions.
- Acts as a liaison between the director and the actors, once contracts are signed.
- Finds replacements, as needed, during production for actors who can't fulfill their contracts.

[sources: Levy, Skillset.org]

If you think we do not want you to get the job, think again! Nothing thrills us more when a talent walks into the audition room and nails the role! Our job is to get the project cast and we certainly cannot do that without you, the talent.

1. What time should I show up?

It is important to be on time but on "audition" time. You need to show up twenty minutes prior to your time slot and be ready when you are called into the room. There is no excuse for being late. If you've never been to the location before, drive to the audition the day before so you know exactly where it is, how long it will take you to get there, and what the parking situation will be like (and remember there will be a lot more people filling those parking spots on audition day). If you are running late, please let your agent or initial contact person know immediately. This is a professional courtesy. When an actor no-shows me and does not contact my office to give me a reason, it will be the last time I invite them to come in and audition. I need professional actors on every project I cast.

2. How many headshots should I bring with me?
    A prepared actor should have their headshot and resume with them at every audition. You should also keep some in your car, in case you are not at home when you get a call for an audition. (You may want to keep a few extra wardrobe items in your car, as well.) It is safe to bring four copies into the audition room. Most of the time you will not need that many but on occasion, especially for an independent feature film, you may have to give one to the casting director, director, producer, and writer, so be prepared.

3. Who is in the room?
    Of course you can expect your casting director and /or their assistant in the room, but you may also have the producers, directors, writers, investors, other talent already attached, and a reader, as well. I could go on but you get the idea – you might have one person or you might have thirty people. Do not let it throw you. If there are a lot of people

in the room, the more get to see you work. What does this mean? It means that you just opened the door to other possible projects! Rarely are any of us working on one project at a time or don't have another project to cast coming up right behind the one you came in to audition for. You could easily get called back for a completely different project and that's a beautiful and wonderful thing to have happen to you!

When it is not just you and the casting director a few things to consider:

- Do not shake hands with everyone in the room, including your casting director! If we are seeing 100 plus people in a day, you probably do not want to be shaking our hands anymore than we want to shake yours and the 99 plus other hands.

- You ask, if not instructed, where we would like your attention or energy. In other words are you to look into the camera, off camera, at the reader etc. You never look anywhere else, especially at your producers and directors. Stay focused on where you need to be focused and follow the directions given to you.

- During your audition, never approach the casting area and never TOUCH the reader or the casting director. Seems silly to say, right? I have had actors try to physically grab me when the script says "Joe shakes Jane abruptly…" I honestly do not know what these actors are thinking but, no, I do not want to be shaken and, yes, the actor was asked to leave my audition room.

4. What should I do when I walk into the room?
Have energy! As soon as you walk into the room we have sized you up and have almost made up our minds before you say a word. Leave the baggage at the door. Don't tell us about bad traffic, the baby-sitter was late, the dog ate your sides…you get the idea. Come in with high energy, smiles and go to your mark. A mark is the place we have set up for you to stand/sit for the audition. It might be an X on the floor with tape, it might be a chair. It will be easy to figure out.

If the casting director has not asked for your head-shot and resume yet, ask him or her how many would they like? The other question you might need to ask is "Where should I put my stuff?" (Purses, jackets, briefcases, etc). Do not just assume you can plop your stuff on a desk just because it looks convenient. I have also seen actors come into my audition room and plop their stuff on my desk… not cool. If you do not know, ask. We will have a place for actors to be able to put their belongings during the audition.

Remember where your casting director or the camera is in the room! It is important how you place yourself. You do not want to give us side profiles; make sure we can see your face.

Make sure we can hear you! Be aware if there is an air conditioner or a heater running or whatever other sounds that may be absorbing the sound in the room and have the possibility to drown you out.

5. Should I come into the room in character?
    The answer is simple. NO. We need to see who you are not just who you are as your character. If you are reading for a role that is pretty heavy emotion- ally, it is okay to come in prepared; we will get that you have mentally done some pre-preparation and we will start the audition immediately. However, when the audition is over, come out of character! We need to see who you are at some point during the audition. One time I was auditioning for a psychopathic – manic depressed, deranged woman for a horror film I was casting and this actress came in, *in character* and left *in character* – we never got to see her for who she really was and for all I knew, she was a nut job! If you are guessing she did not get a callback, you are right. You MUST show us who you are before or after the audition…please!

6.   What is a slate and how important is it?

It's very simple. A slate is stating your name and the role/character you are auditioning for that day. Your slate is the second most important thing to your headshot. Please do not tell us your agent's name, if you have one. It is on your resume, and that's all we need. Your agent might tell you different but my advice is not to listen to their advice. You do not need to advertise for them. You are there to get a job for you, not them. Your agent will get their 10% when you book, that is enough.

Say your name with confidence and with a beat (or short pause) between your first name and last name so we can hear it clearly and distinctly. Say your name with a smile and be excited and happy to be there like you are with your old buddies. We invited you to our home so come in feeling welcomed. If you're under 18, you have to say your age. If you look younger than 18 but you are 18 plus, then you should state that you are over 18 but can play younger. That lets us know we don't have to worry about having social workers and/or teachers on set. 18 and can play younger is a wonderful thing! Once you have finished your slate, wait for the casting director to let you know what you need to do next. We may go right into the audition, chat with you or need your profile. If asked for your profile, that just means we want you to turn sideways to the camera so we can see "your profile". So you turn, wait a few moments and then turn back to the camera and keep the energy up!

Do not chew gum; not even for your character. It will always look bad.

We may also ask you a question. The most common is "tell me something about yourself". Do not go on for five minutes. Keep your answer simple and short, no longer than 30 or 40 seconds. We really are not interested in your life, just your personality, so make it shine with whatever you tell us. The crucial element is to be on your toes and ready for any question we could throw your way. This is where improvisation classes really come in handy, more on this in a later chapter.

7. How do I get past the nervousness?
    HAVE FUN and breathe! Seriously, take a deep breath and have fun! As a casting director I see the audition process as I am "selecting" not "rejecting" the talent. If you are not having fun and enjoying the process it is not worth it. Do not worry about booking the job or we will see the desperation. No one wants to hire people that are desperate; we hire people that are confident. Better to come in believing you already booked the job than coming

in worrying IF you are going to book the job. Big difference.

Here are a few tricks of the trade you can use that will help not to show your nervousness if you really cannot get past it.

- Make your character nervous! It just adds a nice layer to what you have already prepared.
- A dry mouth is an actor's worst enemy. Here's a great trick. Keep a plastic lemon juice container with you (you know, the one you can buy that looks like a plastic lemon?). Just before you go into the room, put one drop in your mouth. You will sour up a pucker for about 3 seconds but then your mouth will create saliva for about 4 minutes.
- Drink TONS of water prior to your audition – it will keep your body from dehydrating and creating more dry mouth problems.
- Put a thin (very thin) layer of petroleum jelly on your teeth. It will keep your upper lip from sticking to your teeth, should your mouth get dry.
- The women may already be wearing lipstick but if not both men and women need to put Chapstick on their lips so your lips don't get dry and white in appearance.

Above all, please come in and just have fun! Nothing makes me feel worse when I see an actor having an anxiety attack over a role that fifty or maybe a few hundred other talent are coming in and auditioning for AND I can only hire one. The odds are against you, right? At some point, if you work hard and do not give up, you will book a role but in the meantime, enjoy the audition process. If you can truly do this, you will see how often you are being called back or booking. We love confident actors, which is different from cocky or arrogant! Don't confuse the two.

CHAPTER FOUR

The Audition Room – Part Two – The Audition

WHAT are the three most important factors for real estate that you've always heard? "Location, location, location." What are the three most important factors of an audition? "Personality, personality, personality." Well, maybe it's six – "Prepare, prepare, prepare!" First of all, we are casting people to be in the film or television show, which means your personality has as much to do with getting the job as your acting chops. This does not mean trying to schmooze us in the audition room – that never comes across well. Be yourself. Be nice. Be having a great day (even if you're not!). Be courteous. Be on time. Be professional. Do not look at me like I'm about to bite your head off; I am a very nice person…really. And I want you to get the job, so my job is done!

1. How well should I know the material?
   Take the time to be totally prepared for your audition. If you have not spent the time memorizing

your lines or doing research, you will not be as prepared as some of the other actors that are auditioning for the same role. We can only cast the role to one actor and you want it to be you! So just like the Boy Scout rule, "Be Prepared" and you will be leaps and bounds above rest. We are not going to necessarily ask you to memorize it, but we certainly expect it. Memorizing your lines allows you to be up, off the page, and have fun during your audition.

However, there is a big difference between "memorizing the lines" and "memorizing the performance". Countless actors make the error of planning how they will say the lines, the way they will gesture, when to take beats, as they memorize. This is a mistake. Your performance will unfold in the audition room. Yes, come completely prepared, but do not come in robotic – it will be boring. Be ready for anything once you get a feel for the room and what the director or casting director want from you. Don't be so locked into what you've prepared that it will throw you off if we ask for something different.

Even though you have it memorized, please come in with your sides in your hands. There is nothing worse than seeing an actor get nervous, forget their line and not have something to refer to when or if that happens to them.

We want you to know your sides so well that your focus is on the character, not on the words. If your nose is in the script, we're not going to connect with you and you certainly cannot connect to your scene partner, whether it is another actor or the reader. Read it until you're sick of it, because when you're sick of it, you've got it memorized.

2. How do I set the scene?

    It is really important to set your scene. That means taking a moment before you start your scene and taking a moment when you finish your scene to make it complete. Using the 5 elements and get into your scene before you even speak one word. Those few moments before and after your scene/ audition are vital. It is important to really absorb the moment after the last line is delivered. Either the casting director will cut the scene or you can cut it yourself but let us know that the scene is complete. You have to have a beginning, middle and end.

    So many actors will jump right into it or say their last line and then look right at me, and I am still in the moment. It shocks me by snapping out of their character so quickly. So take your time!

Remember, you are on camera and we are recording you and a lot of the time. It is not when you are talking when we are watching you, it is when you are suppose to be listening or reacting to the other character that we are paying attention to you. This is very big in sit-com. Think of shows like "The Office"...how often the funniest moments are when the camera is on one of the actors and it is their reaction into the camera that makes us laugh, not what they are saying. We are watching you when you are "acting" and "reacting" – both are an important part of your audition.

3. What if I get re-directed?
    Being re-directed in the audition room is a good thing. I have seen many actors get flustered on the re-direct as if on the first read they did something wrong. If a casting director re-directs you, it is because we saw something we liked! So we re-direct for one or two reasons: One because you almost had it and so we want to give you more information to see if you can give us the full character of what we are looking for or two, to see if you can take direction. Some actors can nail the audition but then when re-directed give me the exact same read. That is not good. It is my job as a casting director to find awesome actors that can

take direction to make my director's job a lot easier on set.

If the casting director is giving you direction, do NOT direct the casting director! Often times, we will direct or re-direct a talent and they will tell us they do not see it that way. We don't care. Do as we ask and do not question what we want from you. Do not confuse that with asking proper questions e.g. you do not understand something in the scene or do not know the proper pronunciation of a word (especially a character's name) –those types of questions are appropriate. There is a big difference between asking a question and questioning your casting director. Trust we know what we are doing, just as we trust you, in our audition room that you know what you are doing as a professional actor.

4. What if the reader gives me nothing to work with? Remembering the 5 Elements.

   Most of your readers cannot act and you get very little from them. As long as you're doing your part and bring on the 5 elements, *(Who am I? Where am I? What is the relationship? What is the emotion of the character? What is the conflict?)*, you will still shine! Remember to make your audition about the other character or person in the room that is reading with you. It does not matter if the reader is not giving you anything, in your mind they are. And really listen to the reader like they are a phenomenal actor! Again, as a casting director we are watching you react and listen just as much as when you are speaking your lines. Listen, think, and take action by responding. Keep the read interesting and we will be interested in watching you.

Eye contact connects the actor to the other actor (or reader). If you do not have eye contact, you are not listening, you are not connecting, which means you are not going to get booked. Be sure to make eye contact with your reader or other actor. This does not mean you cannot look away. A zombie stare gets a bit weird! Remember there are two of you doing the scene and it is vital to engage yourself in the conversation with the other reader/ actor.

CHAPTER FIVE

The Audition Room –
Part Three – Energy

IN previous chapters, I briefly talked about your "energy" and how to use it. Because it is vital to your audition, it is worth going into more detail to help you truly understand what your job is when it comes to bringing energy into the audition room.

Let me start by discussing walking into an audition room. It is your moment. Walk in with confidence. It is your 1-2 minutes in the audition room. Take your time! Do not feel rushed or you will look like you are rushing. You want to give off good energy from the moment we see you. The audition starts the second you walk into the room. Your body language is on display and giving off energy; it's not just about a smile. People like to work with people who are honest, hardworking, and carry themselves in a manner that communicates certainty.

No matter how good of an actor you are, I will not hire you if I don't like you as a person. Do not chance blowing it by having an arrogant mind-set. I want to see how awesome you are as a person and as an actor! All talent has something distinctive about them so figure out what yours is, come in the room and show me using your energy! I will know in about 10 to 15 seconds if I am interested and it all comes from the energy when you walk into the room.

1. What is energy?
    Acting is high-energy. Talented actors are energy gurus. It is defining and understanding the energy between you and your reader or another actor in the room.

    As I stated in a previous chapter, for me, your energy is strongly tied in with your emotional choices. What you feel emotionally is what will show in your energy and you get to decide how much of that energy you want to reveal.

    A great actor is clever and sometimes gifted in making choices to show the exchange of energy between you and your reader. The energy that you reveal to us is also what sets in motion the dialog that allows the story to advance and keeps it inter-esting to us. In everyday life, no matter who you are speaking to, you are exchanging energy with that person, so bring it into the audition room!

Energy is your emotions, character traits, personality, persona, desires, frame of mind, disposition, temperament, point of view. All of these things create energy. Connecting to the energy that you give to us in the audition room is the underlying reason we will want to book you. Energy is everything when it comes to an audition. Help us understand how you see your character through the energy you bring to us in the room. If we get it, we are interested in you.

Start using your imagination – that is where the best energy lies. You have a whole world you have probably never tapped into before, so start tapping! Of all the things I mentioned above, your emotional choice is the most important. Below is a list of emotions that can bring on a great energy. Depending on what piece you are auditioning for will change your emotional choices. Practice each of these emotions at different levels. You will be leaps and bounds above the rest when you become a master of your energy and emotional choices.

LIST OF EMOTIONS:

Agony	Enthusiasms	Offensive
Amused	Envy	Pain
Anger	Excitement	Panic
Animated	Fatigue	Pathetic
Annoyed	Fear	Pity
Anticipation	Frank	Pleasant
Anxious	Frustration	Powerful
Apathetic	Greed	Protectiveness
Arrogant	Grief	Rage
Awe	Guilt	Rapture
Bashful	Happy	Relief
Bitter	Hate	Resentment
Bored	Horny	Revolted
Bubbly	Horror	Sad
Charming	Hostile	Satisfaction
Cheerful	Humble	Self-Pity
Cheerful	Hurt	Sentimental
Conceit	Impatient	Shame
Confident	Indignation	Shock
Confused	Inspired	Shy

Curiosity	Interest	Sly
Denial	Irritated	Startled
Despair	Jealousy	Stubborn
Devious	Joy	Suspicious
Disbelief	Laughter	Sympathy
Disgust	Love	Timid
Elation	Lust	Tired
Embarrassment	Mean	Unpleasant
Empathy	Misery	Weary
Enjoyment	Obnoxious	Worried

2. How do I bring my energy into the room?

   The second you walk in the room, you have to have great energy so that we will want to hire you right on the spot and look no further. Remember about being be prepared; the more confident you are, the more you can focus on bringing high energy into the room. (Not hyper-energy…do not over caffeinate, it will also dehydrate you).

   Remember, the role you are auditioning for as far as your wardrobe. What you are wearing can help you find the right energy for the audition or character. If you are auditioning to be an attorney, do not come in with ripped jeans and a tee shirt.

How can we envision and feel your energy as a powerful attorney when you look like a bum or someone who doesn't care? This is the one time we certainly will judge a book by its cover. That being said, do NOT over dress for the part. If you are auditioning as a cheerleader, please do not bring in the pom-poms! Just add a touch of the character. A cheerleader would dress fun and preppy. A priest? A nice suit would work...not the whole Cardinal outfit (unfortunately, it has happened). Think of it this way, if you have an idea of your wardrobe that reveals the character you're auditioning for, it makes it easier for us to see you in the role and help you create the energy you want.

3. How do I bring my energy to the read?
    Pacing yourself for audition energy is vital. You do not want to use up all your energy in the first 2 lines of your read. If you have done your home-work, make sure that you pace yourself so you have good energy and emotion at the end of your read. Many sides that you are given build up slowly to a "big ending". Rarely will you need to explode in energy on the first line and become blasé at the end.

    Use your hand and body gestures to help with your energy. Be sure to use your body in a natural way as you would in life. Keep it real! So many actors stand there still and don't move. Your physical movement needs to match your emotional choices and your energy or it looks odd. Think smart and keep it real but move! It keeps the energy up. That does not mean you will be able to leave your mark but how often in life do we stand in one place and talk to people? Every day and you are moving your body while you talk so do not be so rigid in the audition room or you will not look natural.

Some of the best acting is in the silence. Silence is golden. Again, do not rush the scene. Take your time and find the different beats or timing of the scene. If you cannot figure it out, hire an acting coach that can go over your sides with you. Be sure to check your acting coach out thoroughly! Ask to see their resume. If they are not booking or have an old resume, I would not use them. Find acting coaches that are up to date with what is currently going on in Hollywood. This business goes through changes like any other business; you want and must come across that you are keeping up with the industry.

Do not let yourself be stiff; look comfortable and that will help you to focus on keeping your energy up. And do not look down at the floor unless there is something on the floor you are suppose to be referring to; looking at the floor gives off a sense of an insecure actor. That is not the energy you want to give to us. Even at the end of your scene. It can look like you were not happy with your audition and no matter what happens, you loved it! Save kicking your butt for when you get back in your car; that's what the steering wheel is for…to smack the heck out of it and take out your frustrations; just do it before you start to drive! Seriously, do not let us see any disappointment no matter what. And chances are, you gave a great read!

4. Nervous Energy
    So you are nervous. We get it. Your job is not to show it. How do you do that? The easiest way is to bring that nervous energy to your character. In everyday life we constantly feel more than one emotion at a time. What I see over and over again, are nervous actors trying to get through their audition and it is excruciating to watch. I love actors and feel their pain when I see that nervousness coming through because what I really see are two actors performing: One is the character and the other is the nervous talent. Unless we are searching for a multiple personality role, this is not going to help you. Learn to make your character nervous. It's okay! That does not mean you play the nervousness up, it just means that underlying energy or emotional choice you have selected for the audition you have a nervous character.

It is important to give your character a reason to be nervous and you can find the back story in every side you read. If you don't see one, make one up. Don't let us see YOU being nervous. A nervous actor, to us, is not a confident actor and that actor we will not want to book. We must know that our director will have confident talent on set. And remember, we WANT YOU TO GET THE JOB! We are hoping and praying you are right for the role because when that happens, it is not only magic to us but our job is done and we can move onto our next project.

Here is a review of a few tips so your nervousness does not physically show. Drink tons of water (not coffee) before an audition. You are going to sweat, so you need to be hydrated. By the way, you do sweat, which means sweaty palms – DO NOT shake hands with anyone in the room! This is not only inappropriate but your handshake can give you away. As a casting director, producer, director, we also do not want to shake 100 + hands in one day. I do not want to have carpel tunnel at the end of the day. It really is about the germs, especially during flu season. I guarantee you if I did shake 100 hands, you probably do not want to shake mine either.

As stated previously and as a reminder, you should carry two things on you: Lemon juice (the little plastic lemon container you see in the stores) and petroleum jelly. Just before you go into the room, put a couple drops of lemon juice in your mouth. You will have a sour puck for about 10 seconds but your mouth will be hydrated for about 4-6 minutes and that's all you need. Also, put a very thin layer of petroleum jelly on your teeth. This will keep your upper lip from sticking to your teeth, should your mouth get dry. Women tend to where lipstick, which is great for keeping the lips moist. Men, put on some chapstick! Dry lips are not attractive for either sex.

Another great way is to not think about booking the job. Think about coming into the audition and having fun! If you are not having fun, I would not suggest being in this business. Life is too short to be stressed out and there is truly nothing to feel stressed out about. You are either going to get it or you won't BUT if you stick with your dream of being a successful working actor, you will be right for something at sometime; just do not give up.

Statistically, an actor gets cast one in every forty auditions. So why not come in and have fun? Every audition you do brings you one step closer to landing a role. Many years ago I started out as an actor and my own psychology that I used was this; when I do land a role, it is going to pay $2,000 or more. So I would divide that $2,000 by ten (20 years ago it was one in ten to land a role). Anyway, $2000/10 = $200 so I would go in and audition and think "Yippie! I am making $200 today!" It might sound a bit silly but it worked and took away my nerves and I did book eventually. All those auditions did pay off in the end. It was like my rehearsals before opening night. So come in, audition and think of it as getting paid… who knows? You still have a chance at landing the role and getting that paycheck. In the meantime, come in, have fun, do your job with confidence and don't think about booking or the audition again. If we want you, we will call you; don't sit by the phone or check your cell phone or emails every 10 minutes. Let it go and move on to the next audition.

5. What is Chemistry?

    Chemistry is what happens between two actors when they do an audition. This needs to happen whether you are with a reader or another talent at a callback. We need to see you connect with the other person. The best way to do this is be very giving to the other talent/reader during the audition. Do not just think about your role. Eye contact and listening is imperative. Looking the other actor/reader in the eye, listening to what they are saying, and react to what they are saying, with emotion and energy, brings on the chemistry. Again, it does not mean you have to eye lock with the actor/reader. We often look away when speaking with someone but, for the most part, look at the other actor/reader. Let us see you are listening to them. Even if the talent does not look at you, do not worry about it. We will notice that. What can happen? You get the job or the callback and they don't. So make eye contact, listen, and bring on your energy and emotion. That is what creates the chemistry between two actors or lets you showcase your talent of being able to create chemistry with a reader.

CHAPTER SIX

The Audition Room –
Part Four – Preparation

YEARS ago, when I was an actor, the thing I disliked most was the dreaded audition. There is not anything in the world that can charge your batteries quicker and get the blood flowing through your veins, like a river run wild, as to when you find out you have an audition. The nervousness and panic within your soul immediately takes over. If you are a prepared actor, all the nerves, pits in the stomach, and panicky feeling will quickly go away.

A prepared actor is a confident actor and a confident actor is rarely a nervous actor. Some nervousness is also normal and it can help you stay focused and keeps you on your toes. As you prepare your scene you will be deciding on the emotion of the character. One of the layers of emotion should be nervousness. As I stated in the previous chapter, do not make it the prime emotion, unless the scene calls for it (then lucky you!) but there is nothing wrong with having a few layers of emotions for your character when you audition. Rarely in life are we feeling just one emotion at a time, so use this to your advantage.

For Film or TV auditions, if you are at a union audition (SAG or AFTRA) you will see a sign-in sheet. Be sure you sign-in and sign-out, even if you are not part of the union.

Do not waste any time in the waiting room. If you see fellow actors, which can happen quite often, this is not the time to catch up on Aunt Mary; save that for a discussion over a cup of coffee not while you are waiting to try and land a job as an actor. Be professional. The waiting room is a place for final preparation to go over your sides, copy or monologue. Stay focused. You are there for one thing; to get booked for a film or television show. Do not let other actors distract you. If you find yourself sitting beside an actor who wants to shoot the breeze there is an easy solution; move away. The waiting area is not time to make friends or keep them. If your actor friends do not understand this concept then they also do not understand the business and should not be there in the first place. Professional actors that do understand the business and what is at risk are the ones sitting in the corner for a final prep or review of what they will be doing once they get into the room.

If there is someone checking in the actors, ask that person, who is in the audition room. Why not? It is good to know if you have two people or ten people and what is their position in the project. Do not hound the assistant, but a simple question is okay. Also, be nice to the assistant checking you in because they are most likely a good friend of the casting director or possibly a relative. If you are rude or a pain in their side, it does get back to us and not in a good way! So now, when you go into the room, you do not have to guess who is going to be watching you do your audition. Something very important to mention here *(another reminder!)* if you are told that the producer, director, writer etc are in the room, please do not come in and try to shake everyone's hand. I mentioned this in a previous chapter but it is worth mentioning, again. We absolutely, without a doubt, do NOT want to shake your hand.

Plan your day! You should know down to the last second exactly how your day is going to go. What you are going to wear, how long will it take you to get there, leaving time to go over your sides or copy, bringing four copies of your headshot (that looks like you now not 10 year ago!) and resume, and print out a map of the location, do not rely strictly on GPS. Get there at least 20 minutes early so you can relax and focus on your audition before going into the room. Tune into how you are feeling; if you have any negative thoughts, get rid of them! Think positive thoughts and positive things will happen to you. I believe this to be true in life in general but it's crucial on your audition day. Your thoughts are what create your emotion.

Let us now take a look at what you need to do before you walk through the waiting room door.

1. How do I prepare for the scene?
    First and foremost, you need to know you material inside out, frontwards and backwards. A memorized audition will always be the best audition. Why? Because you know the material! Once you know the material like you know your favorite song on the radio, you can now build on the character. You will find wonderful moments within the scene the more you go over it and say it out loud.

    If you have an opportunity to read the entire script the better. If this is not an option, you should at least know who are the producers and director. Do your research on them and find out everything you can about the people that have the choice of booking you for the project.

    What if you were the casting director? What do you think you would like to spot in the character? What would you be looking for and expect the talent to bring into the room? Look at the audition from the casting director's perspective. You may find some different and valuable choices rush to your creative mind!

    If you have an acting coach, and you should, book a time prior to your audition to go over your sides or copy. Your acting coach may find moments in the scene that you hadn't thought of. Even the most famous talent still use their acting coaches when they are on set or preparing for the next gig. Your acting coach will become your best friend when it comes to auditioning. Let them help you prepare for what might be the audition of a life time or maybe a nice credit to add to your resume. Do not go it alone. A second opinion of your choices will not only help you gain more confidence but put a final polish on what you have already prepared.

Here is one of my favorite quotes by one of the most respected actors in the industry, Jack Lemon. You should write it out and post it to where you can see it on the day of your audition or even on a daily basis:

"If you really do want to be an actor who can satisfy himself and his audience, you need to be vulnerable. [You must] reach the emotional and intellectual level of ability where you can go out stark naked, emotionally, in front of an audience."
- Jack Lemon

2. What should I research?
    As mentioned previously, research the producers, directors, casting directors, any one that is a decision maker as to whether or not you will be booked for the job. The Internet is an amazing tool to find more information. IMDB.COM is one of the best

resources out there today. Once you see what work they have done, it would be good to rent movies of the work they have done in the past and the type of characters they tend to cast. Or watch their television shows if it is for a cable or network audition.

Or, for example, you are auditioning for the part of a Mafia hit man and this is not your profession, hopefully, then you need to read as much as you can about this subject. Rent films about Mafia related stories. This will help you to understand your character in depth. If you are auditioning for the role of an attorney, you may have an opportunity to ask an attorney if you can follow him or her around for a day to truly see how they handle themselves and speak to their clients or how they handle a courtroom.

Every role you audition for, there is a good chance that there is an opportunity out there where you can ask to shadow someone, living that life style to see how that person handles themselves, which in turn, you can bring to your character.

3. Why is research important?
    The more research you do, the more confidence you will bring to your character because you will obtain a better understanding of your character. The same goes for your producers, directors, and

casting directors. The more research you do on them, the more you will understand the type of characters they tend to lean towards and also you will find out what their "pet-peeves" are so you know what not to do in the audition room. Every casting director is different. If you have an opportunity to take workshops with working casting directors, I highly suggest you start taking them if you have not already. This is the best way to get to know your various casting directors and how they get to know you. You will quickly learn what their personal do's and don'ts are in the audition room. Keep notes from the workshops so you can refer to them and remind yourself of that particular casting director's style prior to your audition.

4. What will the casting director expect from me?
   All of the above. To be professional, have head-shots and resumes ready, to know your material, did your research, walk in and go to your mark, do not try and be our best friend in the room, do not shake hands with anyone (yes, mentioning this, again!), and have a fabulous attitude!

   What we will be looking for when you audition:

   • A part of who you are as a person that will be an element of the character. The idiosyncrasies of who you are will always come into the character.

- Your understanding of the character and how it relates to the story.
- For you to focus and take direction or a re-direct from the casting director.
- The physical appearance relating to the role.
- Your presence, confidence and poise.

When your audition is over, the common courtesy of a simple "thank you" is expected and just a polite thing to do. You should always follow up with a "thank you" postcard through the mail, but NO emails, please!

CHAPTER SEVEN

The Audition Room –
Part Five – Props, Pantomime,
and Movement

EVEN if you have the five elements down to perfection, the wrong prop or inappropriate pantomime or movement can simply spoil your audition.

1. When are props appropriate?
    For the most part, props are never appropriate. Let me say that, again, props are never appropriate! Props will actually distract our eyes, taking them straight to the prop, instead of looking at you. You do not want anything to distract us from your audition. You have worked really hard up to this point; do not ruin it by bringing in pom-poms for the cheerleader role. The best prop that you have are your sides! We love it when we see an actor use their sides as a prop.

One audition that sticks out in my mind was when a talent had to kiss a girl's hand and then kiss her up her arm. Most of the actors that came in kissed the air which looked ridiculous and not normal. One actor came in, gave a great read, and then when it came to kissing the girl, he rolled up his sides and proceeded to use the sides as a prop, by actually kissing it like it was the girl's hand and arm. It was genius! Needless to say, he was one of the few that got the callback.

Look at your sides. If you think it calls for a prop, see if there is a way to use your sides for it. It shows originality, creativity, and wonderful imagination.

2. What props should I bring into the room?
    There is one exception, for me, that is an appropriate prop to bring into the room and that is a cell phone. (Be sure you turn it off). A cell phone is not distracting and it can look silly, especially in the day of cell phones, for an actor to do the cupped hand thing. That can be as distracting to us as the pom-poms. Other than that, leave your props at home.

    Also, think if it this way, if it is something that you would carry around with you normally like a jacket, hat, wallet, purse, etc that will not look odd because we are use to seeing people with these type of items on them.

2. What and when is pantomime appropriate?
Be careful of pantomime. Unless whatever you are pantomiming is going to truly add to the scene, do not do it. If the scene says you are holding a cup of coffee but the coffee is not relevant to the scene, do not hold an imaginary cup of coffee! In other words, unless in the scene you are to spill a cup of coffee on your lap or throw it at someone, do not hold the cup because the script says for you to do it. It looks awkward, especially if you are also trying to hold your sides. Also, most actors that pantomime will, 99% of the time, drop their imaginary prop. If you are holding a cup, be sure to set it down do not just drop it. It looks odd.

Also, when you pantomime anything, our eyes will focus on whatever you are doing; you want us to keep our eyes on your face – what we see in your eyes and how you are delivering your audition emotionally is what we are the MOST interested; not whether you can hold onto an imaginary cup.

3. What is movement and why is it important?
It is important to keep the physical aspect of what you are doing just as real as portraying the five elements. Things like a "thumbs up" can work,

but not if they are forced because that can make you look like you are acting. And in the world of auditions, if we catch you acting, you will not get booked. Acting is not acting but keeping it real. That goes for your movement, as well as your emotional choices. Use the environment around you. The chair in the room can be your best friend! If you use your imagination, you will be surprised at what you can do with just a chair and the sides or copy in your hands. For example, the back of a chair you might lean on it for a nice moment. Also the obvious of being able to stand and sit in the chair creates great movement, if the cameraman / casting director will allow you do move around that much.

The worst thing you can do is just stand there and deliver your lines. It is not interesting. We do not do that in real life. We talk with our hands, some more than others, so do not want to overdo it. Be natural, but move your body! You have to be as physically connected to your character as you are emotionally.

If for some reason the casting director is doing a tight shot on you, then your facial expressions become even more important, keep it real. You can still move your arms and upper body, as long as you stay in the shot, to help you feel natural while delivering your audition piece.

And please, do not take unnecessary risks when you are auditioning. There is no need to throw yourself on the ground or stand on a chair. When you do these things, it just makes us very nervous and we forget to watch your audition!

CHAPTER EIGHT

The Audition Room – Part Six – It's A Wrap

1. What do I do when the audition is over?

   When the casting director has let you know you are finished with your audition, say thank you and leave the audition room. Do not try to create chit-chat with the casting director, producer or director! Leave the audition room respectfully and professionally.

   Once you get home, you might want to make notes on what you feel worked or did not work for you. Actors are the first people to beat themselves up over an audition, so try and look at your audition as an outsider looking in. Ask yourself, "What could I have done more to prepare?" "What, if anything, could I have done differently?" "Did I bring the five elements into the character?" Notes are wonderful to refer to before you go to your next audition. They will help you to remember what you want to accomplish in the audition room and what you feel is working for you. Remember, as casting directors, we are "selecting not rejecting". If you do not get a callback or get booked that's okay. Being rejected is par for the course when choosing to be an actor as your profession. It's the 40 to 1 rule I talked about. You have to receive forty "no's" to finally get a yes! So keep getting out there and keep a positive attitude. It will happen if you stay focused.

2. Is follow up important?
    Follow up is important for any job you may be applying for but it is even more critical in the film and television industry. There is one big difference: do not follow up with a phone call! Imagine if I was to see 100 actors in a day and they all decide to follow up with a phone call? Here's the short of it: Don't call us, we'll call you.

    That being said, you do and should follow up with a nice thank you note to your casting director or producer/director or both. The best way is with a postcard. It allows us to see you, again, and it doesn't interfere with our task at hand and that is getting our projects cast.

3. What is a postcard for an actor?
    A postcard is a mini headshot of you. Do not use a

pretty picture of the beach or mountains. That will not help us to remember who you are! As much as I would like to say that when I see a name on a postcard I remember immediately who that actor is but the reality is after seeing 100 + talent I'm lucky I can remember my own name. A picture is worth a thousand words and we will remember a face…that is our job! Here is a nice example of an industry postcard:

FRONT

BACK

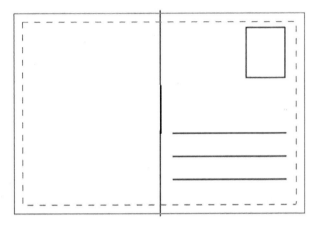

4. When do I send them out?
    The proper protocol for sending out postcards is
    right after your audition. If you do not know your
    casting director's mailing address, ask the assistant
    checking you in if he or she has it. If not, you can
    always look them up on IMDB. (Internet Movie
    Database). Most everyone is listed here. www.
    IMDB.com You should always send it out after
    every audition and don't waste any time!

    Postcards are a great way for you to keep casting
    directors up-to-date with what you are doing, too.
    You should send out a postcard every 8-10 weeks,
    letting us know something new that you've done.
    (If you have not done anything in 8-10 weeks, this
    business may not be for you). Now this does not
    mean it has to be a role you have landed. I truly

believe if actors are not working, they should be in training. So if you have not worked on something, surely you have completed a class or taken a workshop somewhere.

Find a reason to send that postcard out! If you have been diligent on taking addresses after each audition or workshop, within a short time you will have a nice database of your own that you can send out your postcard on a regular basis. Timing is everything in this business and you just never know when your postcard will hit a casting director's desk at the right time. It is also an excellent way to establish a relationship with a casting director and it will improve your chances for consideration of upcoming auditions.

I was casting a feature film a few years ago and we had all the roles cast but one. We had seen 70 or 80 talent for this one particular supporting role and I could not make my producer/director happy with the talent that had auditioned. (I felt we had several to choose from but casting directors are never the final decision makers). Within 24 hours I had received a "thank you postcard" from a talent thanking me for coming in for a completely different role. As soon as I saw her postcard I KNEW she was my gal! I called the talent immediately and asked her to come to my office so we could go over the role. I called my producer and asked him to come to my office, as well. She auditioned and was booked that day. It was a very good supporting role and I would never, in a million years, had thought of her had she not sent me a postcard. By sending it, she came to the forefront of all the other talent and landed the role.

The other thing I would like to quickly mention is that you should also take your postcard and make a mini version of this into a business card. You never know who you are going to run meet. It's considered professional in every business, including show business, and remember, this is a business!

CHAPTER NINE

Improvisation

1. What is Improvisation?

    Improvisation is a tool that can teach you some of the most valuable lessons when auditioning for a role. These lessons are best learned through taking improvisation classes but let's cover some of the basic rules so that you have some idea of what might be expected of you in an improvisational audition.

    Improvisation is the basic skills of listening, portraying, confidence, and performing instinctively and spontaneously. These are considered important skills for actors to develop. In other words, improvisation is making up what you say and what you do. We all improvise every day when we talk to our friends and our family. When was the last time, if ever, you wrote a script when you got up in the morning so you would know exactly what to say for your entire day? Silly, right? Well guess what? You are improvising!

To prepare for an improvisation audition, expect the unexpected. Be ready to think on your feet and keep a running dialogue or monologue. Be sure you keep going and make it look as effortless and as natural as possible. The more you practice your improvisation skills, the better you will get at it. Let your imagination drive you and don't think so hard. Relax. Basically, just have fun; take the pressure and fear off of yourself. You will love it and you will make us love you, too! Why should improvisation classes be on my resume?

2. Why should improvisation classes be on my resume?
   As casting directors, directors or producers, we understand that it takes a certain intellect and creativity to be able to carry out good improvisational skills. We want smart and creative actors on set! When I see a lot of improvisation training on an actor's resume, I will most always bring that actor in if they have a ton of work on their resume or not. I know I'm getting a very skilled and trained talent.

3. What are the basic rules?
   There are 5 basic rules to improvisation. These are not new and can be found in any improvisation

book or class you decide to take. The basic rules are:

I. Don't Deny
    Denial is the number one reason most scenes go bad. Any time you refuse an offer made by your partner your scene will almost instantly come to a grinding halt. Example: Player A) "Hi, my name is Jim. Welcome to my store." Player B) "This isn't a store, it's an airplane. And you're not Jim, you're an antelope."

II. Don't ask open ended Questions
    Open ended questions (like "Who are you?") are scene killers because they force your partner to stop whatever they are doing and come up with an answer. When you ask your partner and open ended question, you put the burden of coming up with something "interesting" on your partner - so you are no longer doing a scene together but forcing the other actor to do more work than you are willing to do.

III. You don't have to be funny.
    The hidden riddle of improvisation is that the harder you try not to be funny the more funny your scene is going to be. Why? Because it's the very best kind of improvisation scene you can do is an "interesting" scene, not necessarily

a "funny" one. When you do an interesting scene, a very surprising thing happens; the funny comes out all by its self. And if you're auditioning for a dramatic piece, you certainly do not want to be funny then!

Stick to your character, stick to the story that is being told or given to you and to stay within the reality of the scene you are playing.

IV. You can look good if you make your partner look good.

   When you are in a scene, the better you make your partner look the better the scene is going to be and, as a direct result, the better you are going to look. All too often, I've seen actors do a scene and I can tell they have some really great idea about the character they are going to play or an idea they want to do. This is wonderful, but guess what? Your partner probably has absolutely no idea what you are thinking and so has no idea how to react. And no matter how brilliant your idea might be, it's practically worthless if the scene as a whole goes bad. You cannot "plan ahead" what you are going to say or do with improvisation, so don't even try!

V. Tell a story.

Storytelling is probably the easiest rule to remember but the hardest one to do. The real magic of improvisation is when we see actors take our random suggestions (like a bartender and a cab driver fighting over the bar bill) and somehow "make it work". If all these elements are going to come together then it's going to happen in the course of an interesting story. So that's just what you are going to try and do, tell us all a story.

4. Should I take improvisation classes?

Yes, yes, and yes. As Forrest Gump once said, "And that's all I have to say about that".

5. Basic improvisation exercise

Here are a few basic improvisation exercises you can do with fellow actors. This is something that is not going to cost you anything but your time. Find seven or eight actors that are willing to get together once a week to play and have fun with improvisation, or as we say in the biz, "improv". I'm not suggesting you should not take classes from the professionals, but use this as another tool to go hand in hand with your professional training. Most importantly, have fun with this! It's a way to starting thinking outside the box and push your-self to creative limits you never knew existed.

Emotional Mirror

Players are in pairs, facing each other. One starts talking in gibberish, with a specific emotion (angry, happy, in love, you name it). The other instantly copies the emotion of the first player, and speaks in his own gibberish. No need to try and copy the other player's gibberish, and both players keep talking, no pausing allowed. After about 10 seconds, the second player changes emotion, and the first one immediately follows the other.

Energy 1-10

Gather everyone in a big circle, squatting down. Count from one to ten, all together, gradually standing up, with increasing energy level. Level one is hardly audible, and ten is as loud as possible, everyone standing straight, hands reaching up.

It's important to watch each other, to ensure you are all at the same energy level. Also, make sure that the increase in energy is nicely gradual.

Alphabet Game

This is a scene consisting of a twenty six line dialog. The first line starts with a given letter (say 'R'). The reply to that line must start with a 'S', and so on, until the whole alphabet has been covered. After 'Z' comes 'A'. By the time you get back to the letter you started with, you must have given us a beginning, middle and end to your story.

Emotional Scene

Think of an emotion (e.g. sad). Play a scene in which the players are as sad as possible. Alternatively, give every player a different emotion.

Character Swap

Two players improvise a scene, and make distinct strong physical and vocal choices. The scene is played until we know the characters. Then the roles are reversed, and every player plays the other's character, in the same scene, same location. The exercise trains listening and physical observation.

Zapping

Four players each chooses a TV format, like the News, a documentary, a sit-com, popular talk show, you name it. You think of a central theme, and the MC will 'zap' through the channels. Miraculously, all broadcasts cover the same theme.

CHAPTER TEN

Monologues

1. What is a monologue?

   Wikipedia Definition: A monologue is when the character may be speaking his or her thoughts aloud, directly addressing another character, or speaking to the audience, especially the former. Monologues are common across the range of dramatic media (plays, films, animation, etc.).

   And, of course, the audition.

2. What type of monologue should I prepare?

   There are two types of monologues you need to prepare: dramatic and comedic. A good audition monologue will only be 1 minute long. The best way to select your monologue is to watch films of actors you feel represent you. Every feature film has a monologue in there somewhere.

   Be sure not to copy the performance of the actor

that did it the first time; make it your own. Do not do a famous monologue such as Jack Nicholson in "A Few Good Men" – *"You can't handle the truth!"* There is no way we will be able to see anyone but Jack when we hear that monologue and I would have my doubts that even the best of talent can top Jack!

Whichever you choose, it is imperative that you are able to read the entire script. If you do not know what is happening in the storyline, you may not be able to understanding your character to the fullest, which will set you up for a weaker delivery.

Stay away from Shakespeare or most of your stage monologues. Although they are very well written, they were written for the stage, not for film. Rarely have I seen a talent pull off a really great Broadway style monologue without going "Broadway" with it. Remember, we are auditioning you for a film or television show, not a theatrical/stage production.

3. Why is it important?
    Monologues are important for a couple of reasons; the most important being that it is going to help you get an agent or a manager, especially if your resume is a little bit weak. Monologues are also a way for you to stay in tuned with being an actor and a way to keep your acting chops alive and well!

I would also suggest having more than one – 5 or 6 different monologues will come in very handy when you start using them in the audition room.

Monologues will be used quite often for an audition. Monologues are a wonderful tool for casting directors to see your talent. It is your chance to show us your best *and we are going to assume that it is considering you picked it yourself, so select your monologues carefully and with a great deal of thought.* If you are 18 years old, do not try and do a monologue written for a character that has 3 kids and has been out of work for 5 years (and vice-versa). Makes sense, right? You would be surprised what I have seen, so choose wisely!

Many directors and producers I work with, have the talent come in and read their sides. If they see what they like, they have me ask the talent if they could please do one of their monologues. This has stumped many talents and, unfortunately, has cost them a callback or a booking because the talent with the monologues had more time in the audition room with us and were able to show us a little more of what they can do.

My favorite site to find scripts is: dailyscript.com/movie.html – use this site to find most any feature film that's out there today.

You will still need to add the 5 elements to your character, don't forget them!

CHAPTER ELEVEN

If You Aren't Working You Should Be In Training

BEING an actor takes dedication, professionalism, and most of all TRAINING! You may feel you have a natural ability, and this may be true, however, even talents that are "naturals" must take training. Think of it this way, if you have never picked up a guitar in your life and I handed one to you and said, "play me song", could you do it? Talent is talent and training is training, no matter if it is acting, singing, or sports. Or let me put it another way, would you go to the dentist to get a root canal done knowing the dentist has had no training? Of course not, and I do not want to see actors that do not know what they are doing either; it wastes both our time.

1. Why should I take acting classes?
    You need to take acting classes so that you can gain the knowledge and skills that are a must if you want to make it in this industry. It gives you a good base to work from. When I look at an actor's

resume I expect to see a lot of training on it, especially if they have not been working or are just getting started in the business. Training is a must for your resume. Your training can easily get you into an audition, depending on the training you have taken. (I will go into more detail on that in the next segment of this chapter.)

Your training needs to come before headshots, websites, joining databases, finding an agent or manager. If you are not trained, you're just wasting your money and time because it will show in the audition room.

You need to learn how to access your emotions. You will watch other actors in the classroom work, as well, which is very useful to you as an actor. Sometimes you will find that you will learn more by watching than when you are the one in the front of the room.

It is extremely important to learn how to break down a character and the prep work that goes into a role. There are many different methods of acting that you will have to choose from; see if you can observe many different types of classes before deciding on one. Not all methods are right for all actors.

Remember, this is a "career" choice not a J.O.B. Any career choice is going to have a financial obligation attached to it. When it comes to training, investing in your career is part of the business. There is a wonderful bond that happens in a classroom. When actors tell "non-actors" what they do for a living, sometimes there is a feeling that you are not pursuing a real career. Actors, casting directors, directors, all the crew, we become a family and support each other. You will find this in your acting classes. If you do not, find another class until you do.

2. What kind of training should I take?
   This is something you must research, depending on which city you live in. You may want to ask some of your actor friends. Referrals are a wonderful thing! Just be sure the referrals you get from another actor are from an actor that has been doing this for awhile. Two green actors selecting acting coaches can put a lot of "green" into a coach's wallet that isn't a good coach.

   One thing that is clear across the board is that you want to take acting classes from acting coaches and audition classes from casting directors. Respectfully, acting coaches have not been on my side of the audition room, so they do not have a clear understanding of what happens once the actor leaves the room. Same goes with the casting director teaching acting classes. Unless either type of coach (actor or casting director) is able to take acting classes or run an audition session, I would suggest sticking to this rule.

I would also like to enforce that you should be taking classes from coaches and casting directors that are currently working in the industry. You want someone who is up-to-date and can help you further your career. If you are spending money on training with someone who has not been around the business for ten years, you will probably get a lot of misinformation.

We discussed improvisation in a previous chapter, but it is worth another mention. If you are in Los Angeles, I highly recommend UCB (Upright Citizens Brigade) or The Groundlings. If you are not from Los Angeles, there are certainly a number of different improvisation groups in every city; you need to do your research and find one.

Be careful of scams. You should not be paying thousands of dollars for a 3 month session. Most good acting coaches or schools will charge $200-$350 a month for once or twice a week sessions. If it is a casting director workshop, they will range from $30-$50 for a 3 hour session or $75-$125 for a full day. Also, watch out for the class size. I would not attend a 3 hour session with more than 20 actors or a full day with more than 36 actors. You have a right to get your money's worth.

Please remember you are taking these classes not to show off your talent, but to work on perfecting your craft. You must be able to take the good with the bad when it comes to the feedback. I've had talent corner me after a workshop because they disagreed with the feedback I gave them. Not that they felt they were right, but because they were worried that I now thought they were "bad actors" because of what I said to them. When you get constructive criticism, it is just that; so listen, absorb what is being taught, then use it on your next audition or job. After all, this is why you are paying for the training, right?

Another thing a good acting coach can do for you is build your confidence and help you with any stage fright you may have. A confident actor knows who they are what their strengths are (and weaknesses) and you acquire this through your training.

CHAPTER TWELVE

The Best Resources in Hollywood & Industry Terminology

1. Which databases should I belong to?

   There are three databases I would highly recommend for all actors to belong to: Actors Access (www.actorsaccess.com), Now Casting (www.nowcasting.com), and L.A. Casting (www.lacasting.com). All three of these databases are used by almost every casting director from independent casting directors to networks & studio casting directors.

2. They are also used by your agents and managers. Most other databases are going to be a waste of time, in my opinion. This is another area where there are a TON of scams out there. Be leery and check your sources before paying out any money to any database company; especially if they are

boasting about the "hundreds of casting directors" using them because there is a very good chance we are not.

3. Industry Terminology

Above the Line. A budgetary term for movies and TV. The line refers to money budgeted for creative talent, such as actors, writers, directors, and producers.

Acting Resume. Focuses exclusively on acting and establishes your credibility as an actor by listing your acting experience and training as well as promote you as an actor to agents and casting directors.

Action. A director's cue to begin filming.

A.D. An assistant director, and usually part of a hierarchy, whose duties will include helping to set up shots, coordinating and writing call sheets, and directing and corralling extras.

Airbrushing. A photographic process whereby certain flaws in a picture are gently blown off of a master print.

Anti-timing. A failing of some actors who seem to be too slow or too fast in responding to action or dialogue.

Apple Boxes. Wooden crates that elevate either an actor, a cameo or furniture on a set.

Atmosphere. Another term for "extras" or "background artists".

Audition. A formally arranged session (usually by appointment through an agent) for an actor to display his or her talents when seeking a role in an upcoming production of a play, film or television project, usually to a casting director, director or producers.

Avail. A courtesy extended by a performer or agent to a producer indicating availability to work a certain job. Avails have no legal or contractual status.

Background. Another term for extras or atmosphere.

Back-to-One. Direction given by the Assistant Director after a take. It means to go back to the position which you were in at the beginning of the scene.

Beat Pause.

Bed. The soundtrack that goes under your voiceover. It may be a bed of music or sound effects or a combination of both.

Best Boy. They are either part of the grip or

electrical department. They are the right hand
persons of the Key Grip or Gaffer.

Big. A term used for actors giving too much of
a performance in the interpretation of their
scene. It refers to expression, voice levels, and
body movement.

Billing. The size of an actor's role such as lead,
supporting, starring or guest starring etc.
Also, where the actor's name will be placed in
the credits and if the name will be shown on
the screen alone or with others.

Biography. A concise account of an artist
or group's industry related experience or
background.

Bit Part. A small part, usually consisting of a few
lines.

Blocking. In rehearsals, actors practice the
required movements, in a pattern or along a
path, for a given scene that allows them to
avoid any awkward positions, such as one
actor walking in front of another actor or
standing with his or her back to the camera.

Blue Screen. Also sometimes called Green
Screen, it is a blank screen, which acts as the
backdrop to live action. Any background
can be laid into the background and give

the impression that the live action was really happening in the context of the blue screen.

Body-Shot Picture. Subject is seen in an outfit (body suit, work-out clothes, dance attire, bathing suit) or performing a special skill/stunt (martial arts, surf boarding, skiing, dancing) that accentuates their body in some way.

Booker. An agency employee who sets appointments for talent/models.

Booking. A confirmed session indicating you have a job.

Booking Agent. One who finds employment for artists from buyers of talent.

Book Out. A call to all of your agents to let them know you are working, traveling or are unavailable for auditions or a job.

Borderless. A photograph that takes up the full space of the paper with no white edges.

Boom. The Overhead microphone used to record actors' voices.

Boom Mike. A microphone on the end of a pole, held above actor's heads to record dialogue.

Breaking Character. Stepping out of the scene which you are doing.

Breakdown Services. A fee-based service provided to agents that offers a daily breakdown of roles for each production submitted by participating casting directors.

Broad. An exaggerated performance.

Bump Up. An upgrade in pay and billing when an Extra says a few words or other special activity in a scene.

Business Owner/Manager. A fundamental management function of an independent producer is making deals, but in doing this there are a myriad of rules, regulations and forms to navigate through.

Buyout. A one-time payment for shooting and airing a commercial.

Callback. A second audition where an actor is either presented to the producer and director or, in the case of commercials, is filmed on tape again for final consideration.

Call Sheet. The daily sheet for a production that lists all the scenes to be shot that day as well as actor and crew arrival times.

Call Time. The time you are supposed to report to the set.

Calling Service. As pertains to extras, a company that helps to book them on extra jobs.

Camera Right. When looking into the camera, your left.

Camera Left. When looking into the camera, your right.

Cans. Slang term meaning headphones.

Cast. As a noun, generally refers to the group of actors performing in a particular production. As a verb, refers to the final status of an actor that has won a role or part in a production over other competing performers.

Casting. When a casting director puts out the news that he needs to fill a certain role that requires an approximate age range and appearance such as a certain ethnicity, height, build or look.

Character Role. A supporting role with pronounced or eccentric characteristics.

Cold Reading. Delivering a speech or acting a scene at an audition without having read it beforehand. Colored Pages. Pages onto which script rewrites are copied.

Commission. Percentage of income paid by actors to their representative. If it is an agent, the amount cannot be over 10% for a union contract; if it is a manager, the percentage is unregulated, but is traditionally 15-20%.

Composite. A type of head shot popular in the commercial industry which positions several different images of the subject together on one 8" x 10" spread giving casting directors a quick way to determine how the subject will look in different settings.

Concept Meeting. A gathering of the producer, director and casting director to reach an agreement about the look and quality of each character in a script.

Console. The audio board or control panel that allows the engineer to direct the audio signal to the recorders, and to combine the various audio components into the final mix.

Consultation Meeting. The interview with a photographer which you have selected as a final choice which gives you a chance to ask questions regarding clothes, make up, what types of look you want to capture, etc.

Continuity. Matching action in each take of a

scene with the same props, dialogue, extras, wardrobe, make up, etc.

Coogan Laws. Guidelines created by SAG and named after child-actor, Jackie Coogan, for the work and pay schedules of children.

Copy. A slang term for "dialogue" or "script" for commercials.

Copy Points. The items in a script that require particular attention, and therefore particular interpretation by the voice actor.

Cover Set. Set which is always ready for shooting on a moment's notice. If a film crew is scheduled to shoot outside, and it rains, they move to the cover set.

Craft Service. The food table on a set, or refers to the person(s) who handle the food.

Crew. Everyone on the set who is contributing to the production, in addition to the cast.

CU. A close-up shot.

Cut. (Film) The director's cue to stop filming.

Cuts. Lines, speeches, songs, or any other element in a printed script left out of a particular production.DAT. Digital Audio Tape.

Day-out-of-Days. Schedule made by the

Assistant Director (AD) assigning time slots for when certain people or things will work on set.

Day-Player. Someone who is hired at SAG scale (minimum) for the day.

Day Shot. A specific scene in the script to be filmed or taped while the sun is out.

Demo. Short for "demonstration," a demo can be a sample tape of a talent's voice used to show his or her abilities.

Dialogue-less Commercials. Used to emphasize a visual image with the spoken words of an announcer as the only recorded sound.

Director. Influences the actions of actors and action sequences during filming, and supervises editing afterward.

Director's Cut. Film that is slightly or drastically different from the final cut that the studio ultimately releases.

Distributor/Distribution Arranger (film). Independent producers are not usually involved in the distribution of films. Distribution is still the domain of the Hollywood-based major studios that generate more than 90% of U.S. box office, but there are also smaller distributors and independent sales agents who handle independent productions. There are also non-profit organizations that can lend a hand in various ways.

Double-take. An exaggerated facial response to another actor's words or actions, usually used for comic effect.

D.P. Director of photography, in charge of designing and lighting the shot.

Drive To. Monies paid to an actor by a production company for driving to location other than a studio lot.

Drop/Pick-up. Term used when an actor is dropped from, then picked-up by payroll; this can only be done when there are ten working days between the drop and pick-up work dates and can only be done one time per actor per project.

Dub. An audio or video copy. Also called a "dupe" (short for duplicate).

Ear prompter. A small tape recorder system which the entire script is recorded and is transmitted to an earpiece through a loop around the neck. It is activated by a foot or hand control. Known in the industry as "the ear."

ECU. Extreme close-up.

Editorial print. Editorial print work involves photographs used to compliment the story line of an article in a magazine.

8 x 10 Glossy Pictures. The primary calling card to the people who will be calling you in for interviews and auditions, and casting you in their productions.

EXT. Seen at the beginning of a new scene description in a script, refers to Exterior.

Exterior Shot. A scene filmed or taped out of doors.

False Start. Term used to describe a take in which the talent makes an error within the first couple of lines. The take is usually stopped, and a new take is slated.

Favored Nations. An agreement which means that all terms are equal among all actors.

Featured Role. A co-starring role where you may have played a large role but weren't necessarily the main character.

Fire in the Hole. An explosion or gunshot is ready to occur.

First Refusal. A request to hold an actor for a

given day. It is not binding for either the producer or you. It is more of a sign of interest than an availability request, and it is not as good as a booking.

First Team. The actual cast members who are being used in a given scene.

Flap. In animation, movement of the mouth. If the talking stops and the character's mouth keeps moving, an actor will be called in to add either internally, at the beginning, or at the end of the line so that the mouth flaps match the rhythm of the speech.

Flashing. What is said when taking a flash picture.

Forced Call. Making an actor or crew member come to work without the required turn-around time.

Generation. The process whereby each time you copy a piece of film or tape it losses some clarity.

Green Lit. The process that follows after a script has been developed and moves into production. Production involves building sets, designing costumes, measuring and fitting actors for costumes, and rehearsals.

Green Lighted. When a studio commits to starting a project.

Grip. Someone who handles, carries, moves, and stores lighting, electrical, and other equipment on the set.

Head Shot. An 8" x 10" photograph that acts as your calling card for securing television, film and theatrical work, showing your face as it actually appears. The headshot should capture your best and most unique physical features, while still remaining true to your actual image.

Heads Out. Manner in which a reel-to-reel tape is stored, with the loose end at the beginning of the tape, enabling the tape to be played immediately.

Hitting Your Marks. The ability to physically stop on a preset mark or put down the product in an exact spot.

Hold. When an actor is being paid, but is not working.

Hold Over. When a director decides to use an actor for an extra day not originally scheduled.

Holding Area. A place where extras are kept on a set or location.

Honey Wagon. A bank of dressing and mini-bathroom rooms attached together and pulled by a tractor trailer to a shooting location.

Hot Mike. A microphone that is turned on.

House Tape. A voice demo tape that includes short samples of all talent that includes short samples of all talent represented by a certain agent.

Ink. To sign a contract.

Insert. A form of pick-up where a short segment of the script is reread from one point to another.

INT. Seen at the beginning of a new scene description in a script, refers to Interior.

Interior Shot. A scenic shot inside a sound stage or inside a set on location.

In The Can. A phrase borrowed from the film business and used in voice-overs. When a good take is achieved, it is considered ready for processing or "in the can." It generally means that the director has the take he wants.

Laugh Track. The laughter of a live audience of

a situation comedy or other television show that actors are performing in front of, that is recorded to be played back when the show is aired.

Lead Role. Considered a starring role in a production.

Line Producer. Concerned with the day-to-day details of finishing a project or just keeping the project moving forward smoothly and on schedule.

Long-form TV. Movies of the Week (MOW) or miniseries.

Looping. The art of matching lip movements and vitality of action in a scene. Dialogue that is added in post-production on a sound stage. Groups of people who work together to provide additional dialogue for a scene.

Magic Hour. The time of day when the sun casts a light which DPs have referred to as magic; a choice, for a brief period of time, during which filmmakers have to shoot.

Manager. One who guides an artist in the development of his/her career. Same as artist or personal manager.

Mannerisms. Gestures, facial expressions, and

vocal tricks that a particular actor uses again and again in different roles.

Mark. Exact locations of an actor's feet on the floor during sequences of a shot.

Meal Penalty. Additional monies paid if a working cast or crew member has not been fed after the six hours allotted by union contracts.

Mike. Attaching a wireless transmitter to an actor's body or clothes to record dialogue.

Mimicry. An actor's ability to sound and/or look like someone else, usually a famous person.

Mix. The final audio product combining all the elements into one composite soundtrack. "Mix" also applies to the act of creating the mix. This is sometimes referred to as the "mixdown."

Monologue. A speech used by an actor to demonstrate his or her ability at an audition.

Mouth Noise. Also known as "clicks and pops." A dry mouth produces much more mouth noise than a damp one. Cigarette smoking also contributes to a dry mouth. The less mouth noise you have, the less editing has to be done later.

Must Join. A situation in which an actor has used up the 30-day grace period to join a union and upon hiring for the next job must join that union as mandated by the Taft-Hartley law.

Night Shot. A scene specified in the script to be filmed when it is dark out.

Non-Linear Editing. Putting scenes together on a computer using film editing software capable of moving them around, and/or out of order, for ease in building a demo tape, or a scene in a movie or commercial.

Off-book. When an actor knows his or her lines and no longer needs to carry the script.

Off-Camera. A part for which you supply your voice to a TV spot or video presentation.

Off-Card. A union actor working on a non-union project is known to be working 'off-card' or Financial Core.

Omnies. In unison, sounds or exclamations extras make as a group.

On-Camera. A part in a TV spot or video production where you actually appear on screen. It pays more than off-camera voiceover, but often requires more work, as well as applying make-up.

On Hold. A situation that occurs when an actor is contracted to be available for the next day's shoot but will not have to report to the set until called.

On Location. Place other than a studio lot where filming is done.

On-or-About. A date which implies three different days, giving production twenty-four hours before and after the on-or-about date to start an actor.

Open Audition. Audition open to the public.

Open Casting Calls. Auditions open to anyone.

Option. Acquiring the rights to a story, such as a current events, true-life story, that guarantees that no one else can work with the party who sold the story. Options typically last for a year or less.

Out Takes. Parts of an original filming or taping that will not be used in editing the finished product.

Overdub. The addition of instruments or voices to pre-existing tracks.

P.A. A production assistant who usually gophers and manages the extras.

Pace. The speed at which a scene is played.

Pan. A very bad review from a critic.

Parent Union. The first professional union you join; subsequent unions are sister unions.

Pausing For Effect. A deliberate pause within or between lines, used by an actor to call special attention to a moment.

Per Diem. Money given to actors and crew when on location to cover the expense of food and other personal incidentals.

Period. Project not set in current time period.

Period Piece. A play from an earlier time, played in the style, costumes, and sets representing the period it depicts.

Phone Patch. A session where the talent and the director are in separate locations. The session must be "patched" over telephone lines so everyone can hear everyone else.

Phonorecord. Any device which transmits sound other than that which accompanies a motion picture or other audio-visual work.

Photo Double. An actor, usually an extra, used

in place of a principal actor who is either unavailable or only seen partially, and never has any speaking lines.

Physical Film Producer. Once you have a script, director, cast and financing, you can then proceed to make a movie. Details and procedural steps will include: setting up a production company (if one isn't already in place); hiring employees or engaging independent contractors; setting up accounting and payroll services, becoming signatory with the talent and craft guilds, finding location; clearing the script and title of any obstacles; while shooting, getting the best performances from cast, crew and director; while watching budgets and time; in post-production, helping to edit shot footage into the story line.

Pick-Up. To start reading the script from a place other than the beginning. A "pick-up" is usually when the top part of the script has been successfully completed and only the end needs to be worked on. Narration scripts are usually done in a series of pick-ups. Pick-up can also be a request to read faster.

Pick-up Shot. Small parts of a scene that are re-shot, usually because all angles were not captured satisfactorily during the first shooting.

Picture Car. A car being filmed.

Pilot Presentation. A one-day shoot to give a network an idea of the look and feel of a proposed program available to be produced into a new series.

Pipeline. A listing or schedule of movie projects in some stage of production.

Pitch. To audition or sell; the position of a tone in a musical scale.

Pitching. The action a producer takes in trying to convince a studio to invest money in a project based on a concept or a script.

Plot. Storyline.

Plus Ten. The 10% commission negotiated by an agent, specifically referring to the 10% added to the base pay negotiated for the actor. (If the job pays only scale, the agent can not take a percentage unless he has negotiated the contract to be on a plus-ten basis).

Points. A percentage of money producers and artists earn on the backend of a film/project.

Post. A short form of "post production." This is the term applied to all the work that goes into a production after the talent leaves. This includes such processes as editing, multi-tracking, music selection, adding special effects and mixing.

P.O.V. The point of view that is filmed, usually referring to that of one of the actors.

Pre-reads. An advance reading by a casting director who is unfamiliar with an actor's work prior to taking the actor to meet a producer or director.

Presence. An actor's ability to command attention, even when surrounded by other actors.

Press Kit. A presentation including newspaper clippings, review of movie, television, musical and theater productions, a biography, headshot and resume given to the media and interested industry professionals. Also called a press package.

Principal Player. An actor with lines, paid at least SAG scale.

Print. Director's cue that the shot was good enough to "print" or use.

Printed Edition. A song published in the form of sheet music.

Producer. The individual who oversees the making of a film or television show from inception to completion.

Project Developer. The function in this role is to write or supervise the writing of a screenplay that can attract a director, cast and financing. If the screenplay is to be based on material owned by someone else, or is co-authored with others, the rights for it must be optioned or acquired.

Project Financier. Upon securing a director and principal actor, production financing is next. Sources of independent financing are family and friends, equity investors, distributors in the form of domestic studios and foreign sales agents, banks, foreign subsidies and tax incentives. A lawyer is absolutely needed during this phase.

Project Packager. When a screenplay is finalized the film must be packaged and financing secured. The film package consists of the script, director, producer, and cast, as well as the budget and production schedule. The budget and schedule are flexible and usually can be changed and adapted as time goes by. However, it is a good idea to have a budget range in mind during the development process. But overall, the fundamental issues of this process are when and how to get talent.

Proof Sheet. After a roll of film is shot and developed, it is printed onto sheets of 8 ½ x 11 or

11 x 14 inch paper, holding up to 36 exposures. Use a photographer's loop to check the lighting and focus.

Props. Any moveable object, from a letter to a sword, used by an actor during a performance.

Protection. You may be asked to "do another take for protection." This means that you have given the director a take she likes but she wants you to do it again to make sure it was the best. Also referred to as "insurance."

Publicist. A person hired to create awareness of a person or project.

Queued Up. Previewing a tape and having it set to start playing at the beginning of a scene.

Rave. An extremely good review from a critic.

Reader. Another actor who is paid, or volunteers, to help the casting office by playing all the other characters during an audition so the casting director can concentrate on the actor being screened.

Read-through. When the director and the actors sit around a table and read through the entire script to get familiar with the story, their roles, and their fellow actors.

Recall. When at the end of a work day, a production company decides to use your services for an additional day.

Recurring Role. Typically found on television shows where your character pops up from time to time in a few episodes of a regular show.

Reel Or Tape. A video tape / DVD compilation of an actor's best work.

Regional. A commercial airing in a part of the United States.

Release (marketing). The issuing of a film by a studio.

Release (legal). Legal document releasing producer from liability, usually refers to talent allowing the producer to use his or her likeness on film and soundtrack.

Residuals. Also known as royalties, these are additional monies to actors (but not extras) for film, TV or commercial work airing on local television or international television stations.

Retouching. A photographic process whereby certain flaws in a picture are covered up or removed.

Rider (to Contract). An addition to a performer's union contract that outlives a special circumstance for pay, and airing privileges given to the production company by a union.

Right-to-Work. Ability to accept employment without joining a labor union, usually referring to states whose labor codes insure that right.

Right-to-Work state. In a right-to-work state, actors who have not joined a union may do both union and nonunion work. Companies cannot refuse to hire an actor because they do not belong to a union or do not want to join a union. This does not mean that a union actor in one of these states my do both union and nonunion work; union actors must still abide by union rules. The right-to-work states are: Alabama, Arizona, Arkansas, Florida, Georgia, Indiana, Iowa, Kansas, Louisiana, Mississippi, Nebraska, Nevada, North Carolina, North Dakota, South Carolina, Tennessee, Texas, Utah, Virginia and Wyoming.

Rolling. Camera have been turned on and film is rolling.

Roomtone. The sound a room makes without anyone in it. Everyone has a different sound, so recording in the same room is sometimes

critical when trying to match voice parts from
one session to another.

Royalty. Money earned from use of the record or
song.

Run Throughs. Rehearsals before the actual
filming of a scene.

Rush Calls. A last minute call by an agency to an
actor for an audition or a job.

SAG-eligible. A non-union actor who is eligible
to join SAG by being cast in a principal
role, being a member of an affiliated union
and having had a principal role under that
union's jurisdiction, or performing three days
of union extra work. Also known as a "must
join."

SAG-franchised. Status of an agent or agency
that has signed papers with SAG and agrees to
operate within SAG guidelines.

SASE. Means "self-addressed, stamped envelope."

Scale. Minimum SAG daily wage for principal
actors.

Scansion. The analysis of verse to show its meter.

Scene Study and Analysis. A pre-audition practice of studying a few pages of a script ahead of time.

Score. The compilation of pages of sheet music that contains all the music for a film.

Scoring. Music added to help fill scenes or dialogue cut by a director during post-production.

Screen Test. A type of audition during which an actor will be filmed performing a particular role, often not on the set or in proper wardrobe or makeup.

Second Meal. The meal served six hours after the end of lunch.

Second Take. Being taped or filmed an additional time in a scene or audition allowing an actor to change his or her performance.

Second Team. A group of stand-ins who take the primary actors' places allowing them to rest during lighting changes and camera rehearsals.

Set. As a noun, the physical design of the stage area within which the actors perform; as a verb, to make permanent the way in which a scene is being played.

Set Call Time. The moment the actor is expected

to be in front of the camera in full make up and wardrobe, ready to begin working.

Set Dressing. Items placed in the scene to complement the story.

SFX. Abbreviation for sound effects. Sometimes also written as EFX. or FX.

Shoot Around You. Shooting other scenes in a script until a particular actor is available.

Showcase An evening of scenes either prepared and rehearsed ahead of time or done as a cold reading for industry professionals who may cast the actors in roles.

Sides. Designated scenes pulled out of an entire script to be used for auditions.

Signator(y). A company which has signed an agreement with a union, agreeing to adhere to all the rules of that union, whether it be SAG, AFTRA, DGA, etc.

Signature Song. A song that is primarily associated with a single famous singer, as "Singing In the Rain" was with Gene Kelly.

Sign-in Sheet. Exhibit E SAG/AFTRA Audition Report which an actor fills out and initials upon arrival at a casting office.

Signing Out. The act of entering the time you exit an audition on the Exhibit E Sign-in Sheet.

Silent Bit. When an actor or extra performs a noticeable or required action in a scene, but with no lines.

Small. A very subtle performance by an actor.

Sister Union. One or more additional unions you join after the first one. The first union you join is your parent union.

Slate. The act of stating your name and agency on a commercial audition while being videotaped.

Slice-of-Life Commercial. A miniature play that quickly identifies a problem and just as quickly offers a solution.

Sloppy Border. A type of border surrounding a photograph that looks as though it were painted on with a paint brush and has an uneven quality.

Spec. Short for speculative. It usually means volunteering your services and postponing payment until a project sells.

Spec Script. Several writers may work together to put words to an idea, and in the process create a script in hopes that someone will buy and produce the script concept. Also, a production company may hire writers to create a script from a story idea that they already own.

Speed. Exclamation that indicates the film and the audiotape are running simultaneously at the correct speed.

Squibs. Radio-controlled explosive pockets of fake blood attached to an actor's body.

Stable. The roster of talent an agent represents.

Stand-in. After a scene has been set for the next sequence of filming—moving props, checking the sound, adjusting the lighting, and arranging different camera angels—a crew of actors other than the principal ones are used to go through the actions that the principal ones will follow, such as walking through a door, sitting in a chair, picking up a object, etc.; an actor who has a similar height, build and look of the principal actor, is used (instead of using the time of the principal) where the principal is going to stand while the crew makes sure that lighting and camera angles are okay.

State-of-the-Art. Contemporary or current.

Station 12. Report which a casting director must

obtain from SAG before employing one of its actors.

Storyboard. A frame-by-frame artist's drawing of key scenes with the dialogue printed underneath serving as a rough plan for the way the commercial or film should appear and what camera angles the director should use.

Strike. To remove something from a set, or tear it down.

Studio (film). Monolithic "Hollywood" entity that oversees the approval of concepts leading to the creation and production of major motion pictures.

Studio (sound). An audio isolation room where the talent performs, with an adjoining control room.

Studio Hire. Union term for actors who work in the same area in which they are hired or reside.

Stunt. A dangerous scene; alternately, a publicity event designed to call attention to a project or a particular actor.

Subtext. The subtleties between the lines of a scene.

Supporting Role. Usually a small role where you had some acting and speaking parts.

Stunt Pay. Additional hazard money paid to a actor or stunt person to perform dangerous scenes. Tied in with SAG.

Synchronization. The placing of music in timed-relation to film.

Synchronization Right. The right to use a musical composition in (timed-relation to) a film or video tape.

Syndication. A popular television show is sold to be broadcast in a local or regional market.

Taft-Hartley Law. A law that allows non-union actors to work under a union contract for their first role. After that, they must join the union.

Take. The attempted shooting of a scene. The "attempted" refers to the usual circumstance in which it usually takes several takes to get the scene right from the actor, director, camera person and sound mixers standpoint.

Talent Scout. Hired by studios and casting agencies to search for fresh star talent.

Teleprompter. A machine placed in front of the lens of a camera on which an actor's dialogue is projected. The dialogue scrolls by and is read when at eye level.

Test Audience. Special screenings used to gauge the reaction of the group, and help determine certain scenes to be dropped and new ones added.

Theatrical Headshot. A shot that captures a view of you from your head to your shoulders. The shot generally does not portray the subject with a full smile, but rather an intense look, or showing attitude.

Trades. Industry newspapers and magazines read by all professionals to keep up with trends and news in the entertainment business.

Trailer. A mobile dressing room for an actor sometimes in a camper. Also known as Honey Wagon.

Transparencies. The slide form of a photograph.

Treatment. A shortened version to a full script which includes a short description of the story and the characters involved, and typically ranges from one to six pages in length.

Turnaround. Cast and crew rest time, from wrap until next day's call time.

Two-Shot. Camera shot with two people in frame.

Type Casting. Assigning a role to an actor on the basis of his or her surface appearance or personality.

Typed-out. The elimination of an actor during auditions because of such obvious features as height, weight or age.

Under-Five (U/5). An acting role designation calling for five lines or less on AFTRA shows. This category has a specific pay rate, which is less than a day-player.

Union Scale. Minimum wage scale earned in employment by members of AFTRA, SAG, etc.

Upgrade. A pay-rate increase, usually from "extra" status to "principal" status.

UPM. Unit Production Manager.

Voice Over. The act of providing one's voice to a media project. Called voice-over because the voice is usually mixed over the top of music and sound effects.

Walk Through. To perform a role at less-than-usual intensity, such as during a technical rehearsal.

Walking Meal. Usually second meal; company doesn't actually stop filming, but food is provided.

Walla. The sound of many voices talking at once, such as at a party or in a restaurant. Also known as "walla walla," this old sound effects term is derived from the idea that if a group of people got together and just kept saying "walla" over and over, it would create a good sound ambiance for a crowded scene.

Wardrobe List. The important list of clothes to wear for different styles of pictures.

Weather Day. If the weather is not right for the shoot and it does not take place, it will be postponed until the weather day. When this happens, you will receive a half day's pay for each canceled day.

Weekly Player. Actor being paid on a weekly contract.

Wild Line. A single line from the script that is reread several times in succession until the perfect read is achieved. Wild lines are often done in a series. The slate may say something such as, "This is wild line pick-up take twelve A, B & C." This means you will read the line three times on this slate without interruption by the director. It is considered "wild" because it is done separately from the entire script. In video or film work, they are lines that occur when the camera is on something other than you. They are "wild" because it is not necessary for them to be in sync with your mouth.

Will-Notify. A call given to actors when call time is uncertain, indicates an actor will work, but no specific call time has been determined.

Windscreen. A foam cover or fabric guard placed over a microphone to help prevent popped "P's" and other plosive sounds. Sometimes called a "windsock" or "pop filter."

Woodshed. To rehearse or practice reading copy or sides out loud.

Workshop. A place for putting together and polishing a production. Also, a place where one can receive instruction and practice in directing, acting, and stagecraft.

Work Vouchers. A paper given to an Extra at the time of check-in. It must be filled out and turned in at the end of the day of shooting to receive wages.

Wrap. The end of the day's shooting of film.

IN CONCLUSION

I hope you have enjoyed reading my book as much as I did writing it. If you get one thing out of this book that I would want to stick to you like glue that would be to HAVE FUN! Auditioning is probably the worst thing that we put you, the actor, through. Do your homework, remember the 5 elements, constantly take training, when you are not working, and enjoy every moment!

The day you stop having fun is the day you should re-think your choice of being an actor. My guess is, if you have read this entire book and got all the way to the end, you are dedicated to your craft and you will be successful.

To stay up-to-date with my film and television projects, you can visit me at www.HelenWheels.net and sign up for the email database. You will be sent information on every audition, workshop, and casting session I do.

See you on the set and break a leg!

Breinigsville, PA USA
12 April 2011
259715BV00003B/1/P